THE METROPOLIS OF THE ANTIQUE AGE
Ephesus

Hüseyin ÇİMRİN

Güney
BOOKS

Contents

Publication and Distribution:

MUHSİN DEMİREL

Atatürk Mah. 1070 Sok. 4/A Yıldız Apt.
Selçuk/İZMİR
Tel: (0232) 892 68 42

Text: **Hüseyin ÇİMRİN**
Translated by:**Bilgi Altıok (Üniversal A.Ş) İst**.
Photographs: **Tahsin Aydoğmuş, Yücel Çiftçi,
Turhan Birgili, Necmi Çetin.**
Color seperation: **Çali Grafik**
Printing: **Seçil Ofset**

1st Edition 1996

A view of agora, basilica and odeum

EPHESUS

The city of Ephesus was first established on the shore of the bay at the point where Cayster River (Küçük Menderes) falls into the sea and on the slopes of Mt. Pion (Panayır Dağı). When the alluvions carried by this river filled the bay, it was moved to the southwest of the mountain, that is, the slopes of Mt. Koressos (Bülbül Dağı).

In the antique age, Ephesus was on the west of the great trade road passing throught the Cayster Valley extending to Asia and it was the Beginning point of this road.

The oldest information about Ephesus goes back to the middle of the 7. th centry B. C., The neighboring Cimmerians who captured Magnesia tried to capture this place also, but they were not succsesful. According to Strabon, the Ephesians moved down to the valley and started to live there under the reign of the Persian satrap Cyros II. During the first years of the Ionian Revolt which occurred between 499-493 B.C., this city was used as a base against the attacks of the Persians to Sardes. The Ephesians killed all the Chians who escaped from the Lade War. Because Miletus and Chios which were port cities leading the Ionian revolt were the main competitors of Ephesus in trade. This peace with the Persians lasted for about 50 years. Xerkses looted all the temples on his way back after he was defeated in Greece in 478 B.C.. But he did not touch the Temple of Artemis in Ephesus.

Ephesus, which became under the protection of Athens beginning from 454 B.C., supported Sparta during the Peloponnesian Wars between 431-404 B.C. and participated in the revolt against Athens which started in 412 B.C.. The Sparten king turned this place into a base against the threats of the Persians in return of this

Artemis Ephesia

ΠΠΟΥΛΙΟΝ ΚΕΛΣΟΝ ΠΟΛΕΜΑΙΑΝΟΝ

ΣΟΦΙΑ
ΚΕΛΣΟΥ

military aid after 403 B.C.. In 394 B.C the Ephesians participated in the Navalof Conon established against the Spartan one. Antalkidas gave the city back to the Persians which was captured by the Spartans again in 387 B.C.. The dicta- torship of Syrphaks and his family followed this.

When Alexander the Great captured the city in 334 B.C., Syrphaks was killed and, thus, a period of affluency fo last for fifty years started. After the death of Alexander the Great, Lysimachos who was one of the generals of Alexander became the ruler and he moved the city to the valley between Mt. Koressos and Mt. Pion between the years of 286-281 B.C.. He inhabited the place with the people called from Lebedos and Kolophon. Although he named the city after his wife Arsinae, this name was forgotten in a short time. During the Hellenistic Period Ephesus lived glorious days. When the Romans defeated the Syrian King Antiochos in 189 B.C., they left Ephesus to the Pergamese Kingdom. Ephesus came under the rule of Rome upon the will of the Pergamese King Attolos upon his death (133 B.C.). The western Anatolian cities revolted against the Romans with the provocations of the Pontus King Mithridates II. The Ephesians attacking the Romans killed even the ones who took refuge with the Temple of Artemis. Sulla subdued this revolt fiercely and punished the city with a heavy tax. During the reign of Augustus, Ephesus was the most important Asian Province of Rome.

The building activities in Ephesus started with a series of state buildings such as the Arch of Triumph built in 3 B.C. and the aqueduct built between 4-14 A.D. made Ephesus the largest and most important city of the Roman Empire in Anatolia.

Meanwhile, Chiristianity was spreading fastly in this city The

The Entrence of Celsus Library

Grand Theatre
The Temple of Hadrian

Romans who were against the doctrins of St Paul had protested him in the theatre of the city. The house where Virgin Mary had spent her last days and died beside St. John who was one of the writers of the Bible was near Ephesus. At the same time Ephesus was one of the seven churches of Asia and St. John had the divine inspiration in this city.

The Goths burned and destroyed both Ephesus and the Temple of Artemis in 262. The city never had her glorious days again. The Roman Emperor Constantinus I built a bath and Arcadius built a road extending to the port from the grand theatre.

In 431. A.D., the Third Ecumenical Council met in the Virgin Mary Church in Ephesus. The Council excommunicated Nestorius and accepted Virgin Mary as the mother (The tokos) of God.

Since the port of Ephesus was completely filled with the alluvions carrid by the Cayster River at the beginning of the Middle Ages, Ephesus became smaller since it was no more a port city or a trade center. When it was captured by the Seljuks in 1090, it was a small village. Ephesus was completely left after it went through a short glorious period in the 14. th century.

Celsus Library
The Curetes Street

THE PLAN OF ANTIQUE EPHESUS

1- The stadium

2-The harbour street
   (Arcadiana)

3-The theatre gymnasium

4-The grand theatre

5-The agora

6-The marble road

7-The Celsus library

8-The Mazaeus-Mithridates gate

9-The brothel

10-TThe public latrines (W.C)

11-The Scholastikia baths

12-The temple of Hadrian

13-The houses on the slopes

14-The Trajan fountain

15-The curetes street

16-The Heracles gate

17-The Memmius monument

18-The temple of Domitian

19-The pyrtaneion
    (Municipality palace)

20-The Pollio fountain

21-The Odeum (Bouleuterion)

22-The basilica

23-State agora

24-The Varius baths

25- The water palace of
    C. Laecanius Bassus-

26- The church of Virgin Mary
    (The council church)

27-The harbour bath

The Varius Baths

THE VARIUS BATHS

The Varius Baths which is one of the largest ones in Ephesus were revealed during the excavations in 1926. Accodding to the findings in hand, the latrines in the baths understood to be built in the 1. st century A. D. , attract attention.

Further there are the frigidarium (cold room), apodyterium (underessing room), tepidarium (lukewarm room), calidarium (hot room) and sudatorium (sweating room) in accordance with the Roman bath style. The Baths were heated with the hot air passed through below the floor called "hypocaust".

The general view of the Agora, Basilica

THE BASILICA

This place with two raws of columns on the west of the Odeum was a trade center during the Roman Empire period where the merchants engaged in commerce and the bankers changed money. The capitals of the columns of the Basilica in the Ionic order with three naves and 165 meters long built in the 1. st century A. D. during the reign of Emperor Augustus are in the shape of bull heads. The statues of Emperor Augustus and his wife Livia found here are exhibited in the Ephesus Museum.

STATE AGORA

There is wide area reached by taking a few steps down just on the west of the Basilica. This is the state agora built during the reign of Emperor Augustus and Claudius (1. st century A. D.). Its length is 160 meters and width is 73 meters. The religious and state meetings were held here in old days and the square area was surrounded with the offices of the various state officers of the city. A few remains of foundations are observed in the middle of the State Agora. These remains are thought to belong to the Temple of Isis which is an old Egyptian god.

ODEUM

The odeum which was a place where the members of the city council, the rich Ephesians and the Curetes met and discussed the future of the city and also where concerts were performed was built by P. Vedius Antonius and his wife Flavia Papiana who were rich Ephesians in the 2. nd century A. D. The thirteen rawed seating places (cavea) on the lower part and ten rawed ones on the upperprovided seats for 1500 people. Since there were no water discharge channels in the middle part called the orchestra, it is sure that the odeum was covered with a wooden roof.

11   *The general view of the Agora, Basilica and the Odeum*

THE WATER PALACE

It was understood from an inscription found during the excavations that the water palace which was one of the largest buildings of the city was built by the proconsul Laecanius Bassus on the northwest of the State Agora about 80 B. C.. This building, surrounded with two storied columns had the function of storing the water requirement of the city. The statues of Triton, Venus and the Muses are displayed in the Ephesus Museum.

The Temple of Domitian

The Water Palace

THE TEMPLE OF DOMITIAN

The area in front of the Water Palace is the Domitian Square. There was the temple built in the name of Emperor Domitian during 81-96 A. D. on the terrace on the west of this square in old days. At the same time, this temple was the first one built in the name of the emperors in Ephesus. The arm and head of a large statue of Domitian found here are in the Ephesus Museum. As it would be observed from a conjectural drawing there, the temple was built on columns. An alter decorated with warriors and arms thought to be placed at the entrance of the temple is exhibited in the Ephesus Museum.

The Pollio Fountain

The Municipality Palace The Doric Columns with Inscriptions in the Municipality Palace

THE POLLIO FOUNTAIN

This fountain with a big restored arch above it was built by the rich Ephesian C. S. Pollio and his family in 97 A. D. With the big pool in front of it, the fountain had a monumental look out with the Water Palace providing the distribution of water to the city water. The group of statues picturing the adventures of Odysseus with Polyphemos after the Trojan War are in the Ephesus Museum, whereas the copies are displayed in the garden of the museum.

THE MUNICIPALITY PALACE (PYRTANEION)

In old days a sacred fire was kept alive incessantly in front of the few Doric columns with the names of the Curetes inscribed on them remaining today. The responsibility of the protection of this fire without putting it out belonged to the Artemisian priestesses (Curetes who had to remain as virgins all their lifelong and who consisted of the daughters of the distinguished families).

They were highly respected by the people and lived in the rooms surrounding the courtyard in the middle of the Municipality Palace. The two magnificent Artemis statues on display in the Ephesus Museum were found on the floor of the building started to be built in the 1. st century B. C. with many additions made until the 3. rd century as a result of the excavations made in 1956 here.

*The Memmius Monument. The
Relief of the Goddess of Victory Nike*

THE MEMMIUS
MONUMENT

When one goes back to the Curetes
Street from the Domitian Square, a
relief of the goddess of Victory
Nike and the remains of a fountain
are observed at the crossroads.
Nike was the winged messenger of
the gods who delegated her to take
victory everywhere she goes. Just
accross this relief, there is a
monument built in the name of the
family of Memmius who was the
grandchild of the dictator Sulla in
the 1. st century A. D. and there
are the statues of the members of
this family on the upper part.
During the 4. th century A. D. a
fountain was added to the north of
this monument.

Heracles Gate. The Columns with Reliefs above the Heracles Gate

THE HERACLES GATE

This gate decorated with the reliefs of Heracles was built during the 4. the century A. D. However, it is deemed for the Heracles reliefs to have been brought from an older building built in the 2. nd century A. D.

THE CURETES STREET

During the period of the Roman Empire, the priests dealing both with religious and state affairs were called the curetes. Since the bases of the columns with the names of these priests inscribed on them were found at the beginning of this street, it was called the Curetes Street. The curetes were also responsible for the incessant burning of the sacred fire in the Municipality Palace. The Statues of famous Ephesians were placed in front of the stores on both sides of the street. In addition to these there is a sewage system under the Curetes Street.

The Curetes Street

THE TRAJAN FOUNTAIN

The fountain built in the name of Trajan at the beginning of the 2. nd century had columns with two stories and was decoreted with various statues 12 meters high. Only the foot of the big statue of Trajan remains where the water flows.

Some of the statues found here are in the British Museum and some are in the Ephesus Museum. Other architectural parts of the fountain are in the pool of the fountain or in front of it. In order to give an idea, this fountain is partly restored as a little bit lower than the original.

The Trajan Fountain

17

The Scholastikia Baths

The Temple of Hadrian

THE SCHOLASTIKIA BATHS

The Scholastikia Baths, built about the end the 1. st century and the beginning of the 2. nd century A. D. together with the public latrines and the brothel, were named after Christian Scholastikia because they were restored by him and, like the other Roman baths, have four divisions. The whole of the interior of the building was laid with marble. The statue of the sitting woman without a head belongs to Scholastikia. On the left, there is a small frigidarium. The statue of the river god found here is in the Ephesus Museum. The second division with marble bathtubs is the lukewarm room and one can pass through a small door to the caldarium. This is the hottest room of the baths and the heating of the baths were provided with the hot air circulating among the brick columns seen on the floor. The other parts of the baths were the resting room, libraries and the gymnasia which had a capacity of serving about a thousand people.

THE TEMPLE OF HADRIAN

There is a frieze of the goddess of fortune, Fortuna, in the middle of the vault supported by four columns with Corinthean capitals in front of this temple built in honor of the Roman Emperor Hadrian in the 2. nd century A. D.. On the semicircle in the back, the relief of Medusa is observed. A series of friezes on the walls on both sides of this relief, of which the originals are in the museum, attract attention. The subject of these friezes is the establishment story of Ephesus.

The Temple of Hadrian

The Temple of Hadrian and the frieze said to be concerned with the myth of the Establishment of Ephesus.

The rider in the left corner chasing a wild boar is the establisher of the city, Androkios. According to the myth, the seers of Delphi made a soothsaying to Androkios when he wanted to establish a city in Anatolia after migrating to the west.

"The fish will jump, the wild boar will run away and you will estabhish a city with a brilliant future there". After Androkios began to travel in Anatolia, he visited many places. At last when they were in this region, the fish had jumped while they were frying them when the oil had exploded, the sparks scattered from the fire with the fish burned the bushes nearby. The wild boar hiding in the bushes began to run away. Androkios chased the wild boar and killed it. So, the soothsaying became true, and the city of Ephesus was esteblished here. On these freezes, beginning from the left there are the reliefs of Athena, Artemis, Apollo, a figure of a woman, Androkles, Heracles, Theodosius' father, Emperor Theodosius, Ephesian Artemis, Teosius' wife and son, the goddess Athena, Dionysos and the Curetes in this order. Across the Temple of Hadrian, there is an octogonal stele (1. st century A. D.) with regulations of Emperor Valentinianus I, Valens and Gratianus inscribed in Greek and Latin about the biulding of the city walls and the state holidays and a Byzantine fountain beside it.

Views of the public latrines

PUBLIC LATRINES

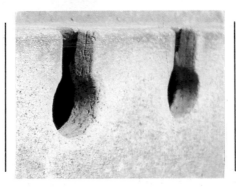

The public latrines were considered in such a metropolis. A water channel connected to the city sewage system was laid to prevent the unpleasent odour in the latrines quickly which was under the U-shaped sitting places of marble with holes. A narrow water channel in front of the closets provided the opportunity of cleaning who were sitting in the latrines. In this place which could serve to fifty people at the same time, the people were sitting side by side by gathering up the skirts of their togas a little bit. The floor around the pool in the middle was covered with mosaics.

A room from the houses on the slopes. Mosaic laid floor (The seahorse and Triton.

THE HOUSES
ON THE SLOPES

On the slopes just accross the Skolastikia Baths, the houses of the rich Ephesians are seen. These houses mostly remain from the 1. st century A. D. which are being restored by the Turkish and Austrian archaeologists. It is easily understood from the frescos

22

The atrium and pool in the houses on the slopes.

paint.The atrium of a house on the slopes ed over each other that these houses which are mostly two storied were used until the 7. th century and went under many changes following their building century. In the part of the houses on the slopes where the excavations and restorations are completed today, the walls of the rooms around the atrium where there is a pool in the middle are decorated with various frescos. A fresco of

Socrates found in one of these rooms is displayed in the Ephesus Museum. There are various frescos on the walls of the room on the west where the floor is laid with mosaics. On the walls on two sides of the entrence door Arhelaos - Heracles and scenes from the plays of Euripedes and Menandros are seen. While passing through a second house complex through here, it is observed that this house has a private bath. When entered

inside, there is an area with a vault where the ceiling is decorated with glass mosaics symbolizing paradise (VI. the century A. D.). On the south wall of this atrium, there is a fresco representing Eros and ghirlands. The washbasin for washing hands and the latrine which can be used by four people at the same time in this building are interesting. The remains of stairs indicate that the house had a second story.

The atrium and pool in the houses on the slopes

The plan of the houses on the slopes

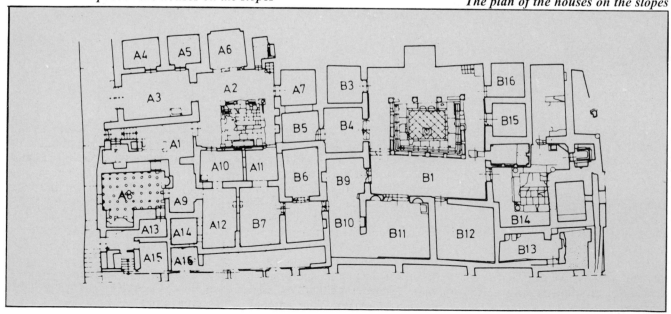

The plan of the houses on the slopes

THE BROTHEL

This building complex remaining from the 4. th century A. D. in the north of the Marble Road and just accross the Celsus Library consists of a number of rooms and halls around an atrium. A bathing pool with two levels is observed when entered from the Marble Road. Through the entrence on the left of this pool, an atrium is reached surrounded by four rooms. The floors of the rooms are laid with mosaics. The mosaics in the smaller room display three women having drinks seated around a table. It is thought that the rooms of the girls were on the upper floor and the lower floor was used for the guests.

Four women portraits are observed in the dinig room. These four women symbolize the four seasons. The most important factors in identifying this place as a brothel were some figures found here and an inscription in the latrines indicating this place. In addition to the erotic figurinesa, baked clay statue of God Bes with the huge phallus was found in the cistern of a house here.

Further, on a label made to show the way on the marble ground at the beginning of the Marble Road, the presence of a brothel at the end of the road is described with symbols and the sentence "Follow me" (ΑΚΟΛΟΨΦΙ) is in the inscription of one phrase.

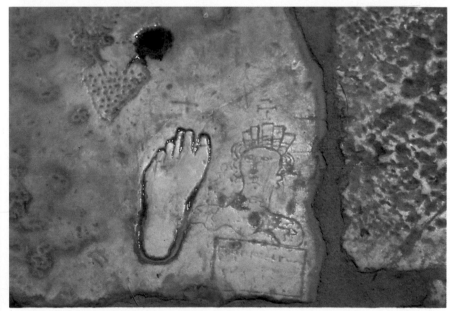

The Brothel and Celsus Library
The sign on the marble road showing
the brothe.

25

The Celsus Library

The details from the Celsus Library

THE CELSUS LIBRARY

Tiberius Julius Celsus was the General Governor of the Asian Province. Celsus who died at the age of seventy in 114 was put in the sarcophagus at the entrence of the agora in Ephesus. His son, consul Tiberius Julius Apuila started to build a library on the tomb of his father. When be became ill, he wanted the building of the library to be continued in his will. Thus, the library could have been completed by the grandson of celsus in 125 A.D.. The library, having 12,000 roll books during that period was ruined and burned as a result of the invasion of the Goths in 265 A. D.. In front of the Celsus Library restored, as the original between 1970 - 1978, there is the auditorium where the philosophers gave lectures and in

The statues in front of the Celsus Library

the cells in the double storied front, there are the statues of Sophia, Arete, Eunoia and Episteme symbolizing the wisdom, knowledge and virtue of Celsus. On the inside, there were the shelves on which the roll books were placed in the three storied niches. Here, there was also a mezzanine floor. Most probably there was the statue of the goddess Athena in the big vaulted niche just across the entrence. The marble sarcophagus of Celsus is in a vaulted room under the big niche in the middle.

The Mazaeus and Mithridates Gate
The views of the Celsus Library,
Scholastikia Baths and the Brothel.

THE MAZAEUS AND MITHRIDATES GATE

Just on the right of the Celsus Library there is the monumental entrence (portico) of the agora, the Mazaeus and Mithridates Gate. This gate, built in honor of Emperor Augustus, his wife Livia, his daughter and son-in-law by two slaves who were freed by them, dates to the 4. th century B. C..

29

THE AGORA (MARKET PLACE)

The agora which was built in the Hellenistic period was vastly changed in the 3. rd century A. D.. This place which was the biggest trade center of the city consisted of the stoa (covered colonnade for promenade) behind the atrium with a wide square plan and the stores behind it. In this agora, connected with the harbour street, the goods arriving in the harbour and the goods brought from middle Anatolia by trade caravans had exchanged hands. On the face of the agora looking at the grand theatre, there are the reliefs of the gladiators.

The Corinthian Column
The Agora. The Marble Road
The Grand Theatre

THE MARBLE ROAD

This road with a sewage system beneath remains from the Hellenistic Period. The road beginning from the Koressos Gate and extending to the Celsus Library is covered with marble. There were sidewalks as stoae for the pedesterians on both sides of this road where the carriages passed. On the right of this street there is a sign on the sidewalk indicating the place of the brothel.

The Marble Road
The Grand Theatre

The Arkadian Street, Agora and the Grand Theatre. 32

Two views from the Grand Theatre.

THE GRAND THEATRE

The enlargement of the theatre which was first built in the Hellenistic Period started during the rule of Emperor Claudius in 41-54 A. D. and it could be completed during the rule of Emperor Trajan in 98-117 A. D.. There is a stage building (skene) of 18 meters tall with three stories. There are 24,500 seats in the cavea divided into three with two diazomae (horizantal passages between seats) where

The Grand Theatre and the Arcadian Street. The Reliefs of the Gladiators.

there are 22 raws of seats in each.

The orchestra is semicircular and there are water channels around it in order for the rain water to flow.

There is a high peripheral wall around the orchestra in order to protect the audiance since the fights of the gladiators with wild animals took place there. The audiance used to enter through the gates on the side. Artistic performances are organized in this theatre from time to time.

*The Grand Theatre and
the Theatre Gymnasium.*

THE THEATRE GYMNASIUM

This gymnasium remaining from
the early Roman period is called
the "Theatre Gymnasium" since it
was assigned to the education of
the players. This building of 70 m.
x 30 m. dimensions is surrounded
with a stoa (colonnade) on three
sides. Just beside the building there
is the bath and there are classrooms
on the sides. The five rooms in the
north were used as libraries.
Various competitions were held
here and the award ceromonies
took place afterwards. This is the
biggest Gymnasium in Ephesus.

THE STADIUM

The stadium from the Hellenistic Period on the road extending from Ephesus to Seljuk, took its shape as its today with the extensive amendments made during the rule of Emperor Nero (54-68 A. D.). Athletism competitions, gladiator fights and chariot races were organized in the stadium of 230 m. x 30 m. dimensions. The seats are on the slopes of Mt. Pion, whereas the ones in the north are built on vaults. The seats, in the period of Christianity, are removed and used in building the citywalls of Ayasuluk. On the west of the stadium, there is the Byzantine bath remaining from the 6. th century and there is the Hellenistic acropolis on a small hill in the north of there is the Byzantine Fountain of the 6. th century on the northern side of the acropolis.

The Stadium.

The Arcadiana Street

THE HARBOUR STREET (ARCADIANA)

The marble street extending between the grand theatre and the harbour is 11 meters wide and 530 meters long. Underneath this street which was built during the Hellenistic Period and where many kings and emperors were welcomed there is the big sewage channel extending to the harbour. This street is named after Emperor Arcadius (395-408) because it was repaired during his rule. There are two monumental porticoes on both ends of the street and roofed colonnades and stores on both sides.Four big columns were placed on this street during the 6. the century. It is said for the statues of the four apostles who were the writers of the Bible to be on these columns before.

The Church of Virgin Mary

THE CHURCH OF VIRGIN MARY (The Council Church)

A footpath just on the left of the exit of Ephesus leads to the Church of Virgin Mary. The churches have a prominant place in the history of Ephesus due to the councils met here in 431 and 439. During the council met on the date of June 22, 431, Virgin Mary, Christ and whether Christ was the son of God were discussed. The Patriarch of Üstanbul, Nestorius, attracted all the fury and was banished by saying that Christ was not the son of God but only an exulted person. The Council decided that Christ had one personality and two identities and that Virgin Mary was really the mother of God. This church was used as an education center for the training of the Ephesian priests. It is the first church built in the name of Virgin Mary. The Pope, Paul IV, who came to Ephesus in 1967 prayed in this church.

THE HARBOUR BATHS

These baths understood to have been built in the 2. nd cenury A. D. were amended during the rule of Emperor Constantius (317-361) in the 4. th century and were named as the "Constantius Baths" after him. There is a frigidarium in the middle of the somewhat rectangular hall on the east of the building and there are undressing rooms on both sides of the hall. The caldarium of the baths is a wide hall on the west of the frigidarium. The remains of the heating system (hypocaust) are seen underneath this hall.

The Harbour Baths
The Hypocaust System of the Harbour Baths

The Artemision

The Temple of Artemis (Reconstruction)

ARTEMISION (THE TEMPLE OF ARTEMIS)

The Temple of Artemis which was considered as one of the Seven Wonders of the World by the writers of the antique world was built in the southwest of the hill called Ayasuluk. Today, only a few pieces of marble and a singlecolumn are seen there.

The source of the Artemis cult goes back to Cybele, the mother goddess of Anatolia. The Artemis of Ephesus bears many features of this very old and, at the same time, extremely interesting Anatolian mother goddess. During the excavations, four building phases going back to the 8. th century B. C. other than the present one were identified. The temple of Artemis was built according to the plans of architect Chersiphron from Crete and his son Metagenes during the first half of the 6. th century B. C. on older temples. On the western side of this temple with the dimensions of 55 m. x 110 m. there are columns with their drums decorated with reliefs given as gift by the Lydian King Croesus.

About two hundred years later after the building of this temple it was burned by a lunatic called Herostratos, who wanted to be mentioned in history, on the night when Alexander the Great was born (356 B. C.). The Ephesians decided to built a larger and more magnificient temple in place of the burned one. The new temple was started to be built on a platform of 3 meters high by the architect Cheirocrates.

Alexander the Great wanted to give financial aid to the temple which was not completed in 334 B. C. because it was burned on the night he was born. But the proud Ephesians refused this offer with great dignity by saying, "How can a god help to antoher god?" Although the Temple of Artemis of Ephesus was rebuilt after it was looted and destructed with the invasion of the Goths in 263 A. D., the temple lost its importance as a result of the spread of Christianity and its remains were used as building material for many buildings for centuries.

During the excavations made between the years of 1869-1874 by the English engineer J. T. Wood and the excavations made by D. G. D. G. Hogarth for the British Museum between the years of 1904-1905 many pieces were sent to England and a few to the Istanbul Archaeological Museum.

The Fortification Walls of the Church of St. John . The Church of St. John

THE CHURCH OF ST. JOHN

St. John came to Ephesus in 42 A. D. with Virgin Mary. They both had the aim of spreading the belief of Christianity which emerged in Jerusalem. Especially St. Paul, who came to the city in 53 A. D. succeeded in forming a Christian society with his preachings who stayed here for three years. Meanwhile, St. John was tortured in Rome where he went. Upon these tortures, St. John who wrote

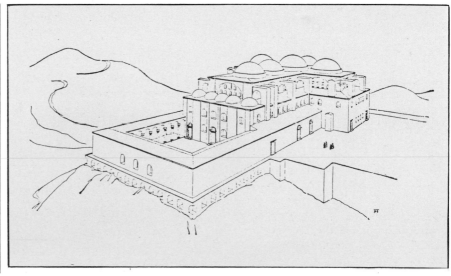

The Church of St. John and the fortifications. Baptisterium

the Apocalypse returned to the city where he lived and died in a short time. First, a church with a wooden roof was built during the 4. th century A. D. in the place where a monument was erected in order to indicate the location of his grave. Later, Emperor Justinian built this basilica with a dome of which the remains came to our day and a new habitation area had formed in the vicinity. The building with a cross plan is entered through a courtyard called the atrium. From the atrium, the narthex on the east is reached and the middle nave of the basilica is reached from there. The middle nave and the transept are covered by six domes. There are the

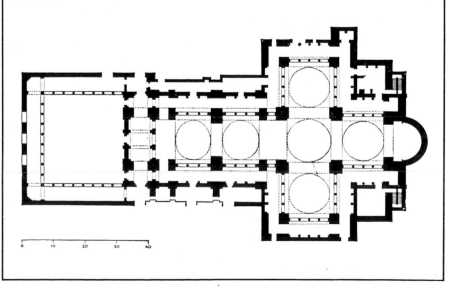

Die Grabkammer des Heiligen Johannes und Grundriss der Johanneskirche

galleries extending from the narthex to the apsis above the side naves. The tomb of St. John is underneath the domed part in the middle. It is believed for the dust coming from the hole of the tomb to have healing powers. In the hall in the northeast of the church, there is a baptistry. The small chapel in the north of the tomb of St. John is decorated with frescoes remaining from the 10. th century picturing Christ in the middle with St. John on the left and a priest on the right. The aqueducts just beside the Church of St. John remain from the Byzantine period.

The Church of St. John.

DThe İsabey Mosque and its
courtyard. Marble Works

İSABEY MOSQUE

When looked down from the Church of St. John, the valley filled by Cayster river in centuries is seen.

At the beginning of this valley there is the İsabey Mosque built by Aydınoğlu İsa Bey in 1375. The door on the western face covered with marble attracts attention with its decorations. There are minarets beside the eastern and western doors of the mosque. Today, only the minaret built from brick beside

the western door is partly erect. When entered through this door, the courtyard with a fountain in the middle surrounded by collonades on three sides is reached. It is assumed for the colonnades where antique columns were used to have been covered with two domes of 9 m diameters supported by four granite columns. The tops of the windows are decorated with different elements.

Besides, the remains of the Saadet Hatun Baths remaining from the 14. th century a little far from the mosque attract attention.

The Entrence of the İsabey Mosque.   46

EPHESUS MUSEUM

Most of the objects displayed in the Museum which has moved to the new building in 1964 consists of the pieces found during the excavations carried on since 1863.

In the first hall of the museum, the findings from the houses on the slopes in Ephesus are displayed. In the display cases here, such findings as the lamps of the Greek and Roman periods, vases, the heads of Bes and Hermes, Eros heads made of bronze and marble, the head of Socrates and his fresco are on exhibiton. In the second hall, the statues of the Pholio and Trajan Fountains are observed.

In the third small hall following the courtyard, there are tomb findings and statues of Cybele, the first mother goddess of Anatolia.

In the room following the hall of the tomb findings, there are three Artemis statues of various sizes and the findings from the Temple of Artemis. There is no doubt that the finding which attracts most attention is the Artemis statue made of marble dating to the 1. st century A. D. found in the Prytaneion in Ephesus. The goddess is standing and fully dressed.

There is a headscarf attached to her head with a cylindirical ring and a crown with three stories decorated with griffons and sphinxes. It is possibleto see the Temple of Artemis in this crown. There is a sweet serious expression on the face of the statue.

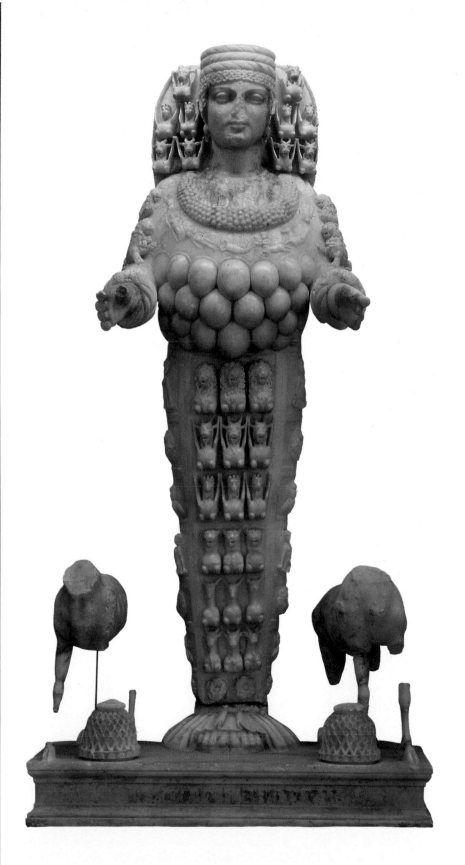

The Statue of Artemis 1. st century A. D.

The head of Sokrates 1. st century A. D.   48

The Resting Warrior ,1. st century A. D. The Figure of God Bes ,2. nd century A. D.

The eyebrows are a little bit austere and the eyes are almond shaped. The full lips are closed.

The neck is thick and decorated with a neclace. Her chest is covered with symbols of fertility in the shape of eggs. The skirt is dividid into sections.

Each section is full of reliefs of sacred animals. The rim of the

The Statue of Aphrodite, 2. nd century A. D. The Statue of Dionyssos, 2.nd century A. D. The friezes of the Temple of Hadrian.

dress is constricted with a bind. Only the tips of the toes are seen.

In the hall at the far end of the museum, there are the friezes of the Temple of Hadrian, the statues of the Emperor Domitian, Emperor Augustus and his wife. Besides, an alter found in the Temple of Domitian is also here.

The statues of the Leacanius Bassus Fountaini. The

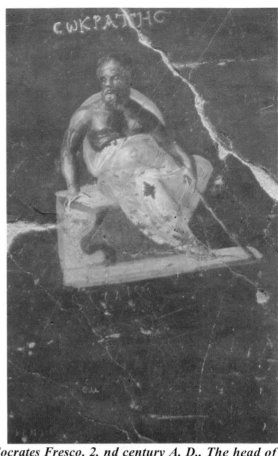

The Socrates Fresco, 2. nd century A. D.. The head of

Polyphemos Group ,1. st century B. C.

Lysymaches, 1.st century B.C..

The ivory frieze, 2. nd century A. D.

The House of Virgin Mary.
The Sacred Fountains.

by the Moslems as well as the Christians and votive offerings are made.

It is believed for the waters flowing from the fountains here to be healing and curing the sick. There is a pool in the north of the house about 100 meters far. Every year, rites in commemoration of Virgin Mary is carried on,the 15. th day of August.

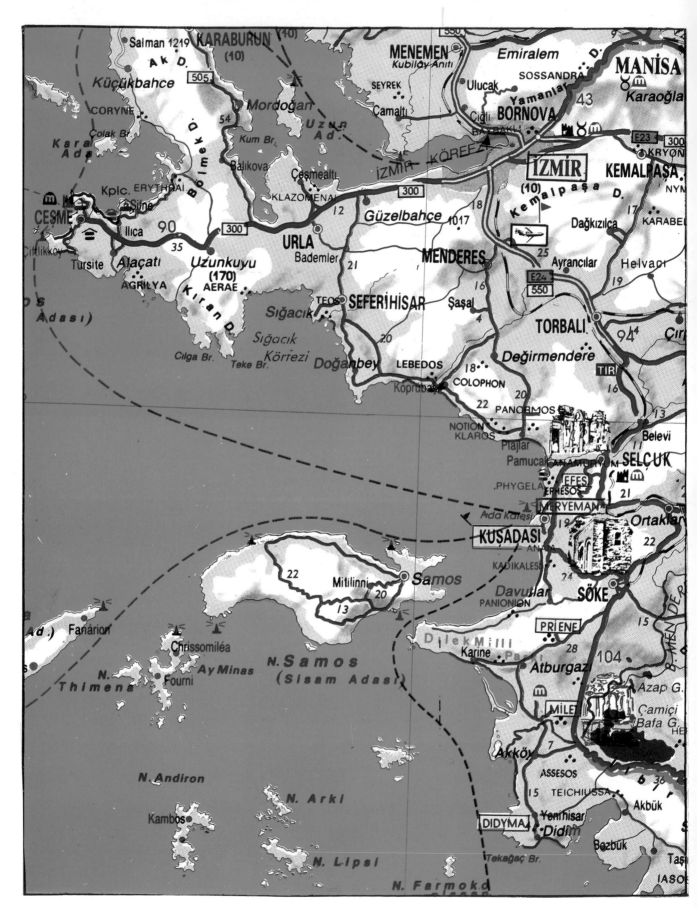